THIS BOOK
BELONGS TO

To Dad,
Thanks for everything.

Published by Little Lotl Books
First Edition 2019
Text and illustrations copyright © Lucia Paganini, 2019
www.lucisaurus.com

ISBN: 978-1-9161060-1-7

DAD'S SECRET:
il segreto di papà

AMAZING
DAD

★ BEST DADDY EVER ★

best
DAD

This is Daddy.
Daddy is a species of Father
who can do many things.

Questo è papà Dario.
Papà Dario è un esemplare di
papà che sa fare tante cose.

During the day, he is an excellent chef.

Durante il giorno è un ottimo cuoco.

He is not bad as a cleaner either.

Non è niente male anche come addetto alle pulizie.

BEST DAD
BEST DAD

In his spare time, he gains
experience as a doctor.

*Nel tempo libero ha
maturato esperienza
come dottore.*

He is also very good as a comedian.

Se la cava molto bene pure a fare il comico.

If the fun isn't enough, he can
transform into a slide.

*Se il divertimento non è
abbastanza, si può trasformare
in uno scivolo.*

Sometimes he also
works as a banker.

*Qualche volta lavora
anche in banca.*

During the night, he
learnt to be a singer
and a night watchman.

*Di notte ha imparato
a fare il cantante e la
guardia notturna.*

He also does a
great job as a taxi
driver and his fares
are very competitive.

Fa un ottimo lavoro anche
come tassista e le sue tariffe
sono molto competitive.

FREE

But how does a species of
Father do all these things?

*Ma come fa un esemplare di
papà a fare tutte queste cose?*

Well... He is a superhero!

Beh... lui è un supereroe!

Our superhero.

Il nostro supereroe.

DAD
PAPÁ

PAPÀ
DAD

This is a picture of my daddy!
Questo è un disegno del mio papà!